A PERSONAL TOUR OF PEOPLE MANAGEMENT

A Career Syllabus

Cyriel Godderie

authorHOUSE®

AuthorHouse™
1663 Liberty Drive, Suite 200
Bloomington, IN 47403
www.authorhouse.com
Phone: 1-800-839-8640

First published by AuthorHouse 4/20/2009

ISBN: 978-1-4389-6282-5 (sc)

Printed in the United States of America
Bloomington, Indiana

This book is printed on acid-free paper.

INTRODUCTION

Being a great believer in my own fifty percent rule - which states that I take no more than fifty percent of the credit for everything that goes right in my life and at least fifty percent for everything that goes wrong – I would like to share the following with the reader and student:

Fifty percent of what I picked up - and share here with you - about people management, I learned through my successes, from the recompenses, encouragement and coaching of my many great bosses and mentors, from the compliments and constructive criticism of the excellent people who worked with me (and who were often much better than me), from the fine seminars I attended and the good books I read.

The other fifty percent I learned from the things I should have done and did not do, from the things I did and should not have done, from my failures, from hiring the wrong people, from hesitating to fire the wrong people, from promoting the wrong people, from criticism I received during exit interviews.

Communication is a two-way process. That is why I only used the left pages for my remarks, observations and annotations. On the right side I left ample space for your notes, your thoughts, your comments, your own practices and your own experiences. I hope you will share these with me too.

Federico Fellini once said that a movie is like real life with all the dull moments cut out. This syllabus is like a real book with all the dull stuff cut out.

All royalties received from the sale of this syllabus I pledge to donate to education foundation charities of my choice.

Cyriel Godderie

DEDICATION

For Raymond Wolff.

For Joris and Suzanne Onzea.

For Barry Sealey, who opened the wide world for me.

For Walt Rakowich, who closed it for me with superb elegance.

If you think you are a flyer
marry a person who won't clip your wings

CONTENTS

MANAGING YOU

Tour stop 1

You are the only thing which you completely own:

If you can not supervise yourself, there is no hope that you could possibly supervise anything or anyone else.

You can only take responsibility for other people when you have proven you can take responsibility for yourself.

Manage yourself:

No excessive drinking: drink with moderation. Keep your intake down at company functions. Don't drink and drive. Don't drink and manage.

No drug abuse: that goes of course for illegal drugs, but also for legal and prescription drugs.

No smoking, stop smoking, it is no longer cool. It is detrimental to your health.

No compulsive spending. That goes for company expenses, for sure, but also for personal spending. Money problems create excessive stress (of the very bad kind).

Sleep enough and learn to take naps.

HOW CAN YOU POSSIBLY MANAGE OTHER PEOPLE IF YOU CANNOT MANAGE YOURSELF ?

Your notes, thoughts and comments

_____

_____

_____

_____

_____

_____

_____

_____

_____

_____

_____

_____

_____

_____

_____

_____

_____

_____

_____

_____

_____

_____

_____

_____

_____

_____

_____

_____

Tour stop 2

Whatever you think of your capabilities and expertise; without luck nothing much is possible, without luck you are not going to go anywhere fast.

Of course you can push your luck with hard work and great courage:

- Hard work *is to be at the station*
- Luck *is trains coming by*
- Courage *is dare to take a train*

When you take a train, make sure it is a People Express: Whatever you think of your competence or knowledge; without people management skills nothing much is possible, without people management skills you are not going to go anywhere fast.

YOU HAVE TO BE LUCKY

Your notes, thoughts and comments

_____

_____

_____

_____

_____

_____

_____

_____

_____

_____

_____

_____

_____

_____

_____

_____

_____

_____

_____

_____

_____

_____

_____

_____

_____

_____

_____

_____

_____

_____

_____

Tour stop 3

What is the right company to be in?

A company that is lean, mean and flat. (*Which is a company that does not go easily bust when the economic cycle turns down*).

A company that invests in its associates, that keeps their skills current, that provides them with opportunities to try new things, that assigns them to projects they learn from, that offers them scope for self-development and continuous improvement.

A company that has gone to performance-based compensation.

A company that offers many possibilities for salary and responsibility promotions on a lateral, rather than a vertical basis.

A company that is not afraid of hiring people who are very well connected through the internet; people who, if it does not match their expectations, can tell legions with one click of the mouse.

A company that can integrate four generations (veterans, boomers, Xers and Yers), working side-by-side.

A company that treats its people the way they do customers.

DON'T BE IN THE WRONG COMPANY

Your notes, thoughts and comments

_____

_____

_____

_____

_____

_____

_____

_____

_____

_____

_____

_____

_____

_____

_____

_____

_____

_____

_____

_____

_____

_____

_____

_____

_____

_____

_____

_____

Tour stop 4

What is the right job to have?

- A job which is compatible with your sensibilities
- A job which allows you to be yourself; it is extremely stressful to fake who you are not all the time.
- A job which is compatible with your natural skills.
- A job which you can learn from.
- A job which provides opportunities to try new things.
- A job which is in line with your professional expertise.
- A job which fills you with enthusiasm.
- A job which excites you
- A job which lets you work with friends.
- A job which provides occasions for fun.
- A job which you love.
- A job which you don't want to lose.

If any of the afore mentioned is not true at some level, don't settle.

Move on.

How do you find the right job?

You take one job, discover what you like and don't like about it, find out what you are good and bad at, and then you change jobs to get closer to the right fit.

DON'T HAVE THE WRONG JOB

Your notes, thoughts and comments

_____

_____

_____

_____

_____

_____

_____

_____

_____

_____

_____

_____

_____

_____

_____

_____

_____

_____

_____

_____

_____

_____

_____

_____

_____

_____

_____

_____

Tour stop 5

A great boss to work for is a successful boss.

A great boss to work for is one who also works for you:

- A boss who aligns your ambitions with his and with the company's.
- A boss you love to work with and for.
- A boss who coaches you.
- A boss you can talk to.
- A boss who is approachable.
- A boss who supports you.
- A boss who delegates to you.
- A boss who trains you, develops you.
- A boss who stretches you.
- A boss who is tough but fair.

Not every boss is going to be a great boss. Even if you are very lucky, chances are you are going to work for a bad boss at least a couple of times during your professional career.

Try to get away from that person as soon as you can manage it. In the meantime, while you are suffering, try to make the best of it by learning how <u>not</u> to do things.

If you hit a bad boss twice in a row, you are either very unlucky or the time has come to ask yourself a question: Is it maybe me?

If you hit a bad boss three times in a row, the time has definitely come to answer the question: Yes, it is probably me!!

Don't work for the wrong boss

Your notes, thoughts and comments

_____
_____
_____
_____
_____
_____
_____
_____
_____
_____
_____
_____
_____
_____
_____
_____
_____
_____
_____
_____
_____
_____
_____
_____
_____
_____
_____
_____

Tour stop 6

There is nothing like being unemployment-proof anymore, but you can still work hard at being unemployment-resistant.

When you develop the following skills and abilities, you will consolidate your job, and/or increase your employability, and/or find another job quickly if and when needed:

- People management skills
- Finance and Management Accounting skills
- Ability to work in ambiguous, complex and uncertain situations
- Ability to make effective decisions when there is no one right answer
- Ability to solve problems
- High levels of interpersonal skills, such as persuasion and influencing

Seek to make lateral promotions in between vertical ones:

- It widens your knowledge base and expertise
- It consolidates your employability

Widen your horizons:

- Take on an assignment abroad.
- Learn to speak fluently at least one foreign language.

IT IS GOOD TO BE EMPLOYED
IT IS EVEN BETTER TO BE EMPLOYABLE

Your notes, thoughts and comments

_____

_____

_____

_____

_____

_____

_____

_____

_____

_____

_____

_____

_____

_____

_____

_____

_____

_____

_____

_____

_____

_____

_____

_____

_____

_____

_____

Tour stop 7

Don't keep your eye on the next promotion, or the next job; instead keep your nose to the grindstone, do your work well, work hard and look for more work all the time.

Do deliver sensational performance in your present job.

Expand your present job beyond its official boundaries. You won't know if you have stepped over the line until you have done it. Until somebody tells you to take a step back, you have not crossed the line.

Don't just do the predictable, expand your job's horizons to include bold and unexpected activities.

If you do all that and more, with that little bit of luck, you will be at the station, trains will come along, and you will have the confidence to step on a the train of your choice.

WHEN YOU ARE OUT OF WORK,
LOOK FOR A JOB
WHEN YOU HAVE A JOB,
LOOK FOR MORE WORK

Your notes, thoughts and comments

_____

_____

_____

_____

_____

_____

_____

_____

_____

_____

_____

_____

_____

_____

_____

_____

_____

_____

_____

_____

_____

_____

_____

_____

Tour stop 8

Whatever your capabilities are, whatever your professional expertise is, whatever your technology skills are, whatever your internet skills are, you are incomplete, unfinished and deficient without finance and management accounting skills

You don't have to be a MBA but you do have to have a very thorough understanding of finance and management accounting concepts:

Can you read, evaluate and interpret financial statements?

- The balance sheet
- The income statement
- The cash flow statement
- The funds flow statement
- …

Do you know how to do the following?

- Financial analysis
- Calculate future and present value
- Discount and compound
- Measuring cash flows
- Capital budgeting
- …
- …

LEARN FINANCE AND MANAGEMENT ACCOUNTING SKILLS

Your notes, thoughts and comments

_____
_____
_____
_____
_____
_____
_____
_____
_____
_____
_____
_____
_____
_____
_____
_____
_____
_____
_____
_____
_____
_____
_____
_____
_____
_____
_____
_____
_____
_____

Tour stop 9

Numeracy is different from being wired and connected; it is different from internet, computer and technology know-how.

You may like flying, but you cannot fly blind: You need gauges and the information they supply.

Non-financial problems always have a finance side.

Every problem and opportunity has a numerical aspect.

All solutions are number-oriented.

Planning, forecasting and budgeting

Are you interested in numbers?

Do you have a number wise mind?

Do you like to play with numbers?

Do you know where to dig up dependable information?

Do you use numbers with confidence?

How are your statistical techniques?

Can you interpret possibilities, probabilities and expectations?

Calculating averages and moving averages?

Converting numbers into trends?

Can you bring numbers to life with ratios?

Are your basic math skills intact?

…

INNUMERACY IS A CAREER STOPPER

Your notes, thoughts and comments

_____
_____
_____
_____
_____
_____
_____
_____
_____
_____
_____
_____
_____
_____
_____
_____
_____
_____
_____
_____
_____
_____
_____
_____
_____
_____
_____
_____

TOUR STOP 10

Ask yourself: What is the worst that can possibly happen?
Prepare yourself to accept the worst.
Work calmly and methodically to improve upon the worst.

When you can't change the world, you can learn to change your response to it.

There are three things that are not worth worrying about:

The unimportant: very few things are very important. Just clean out your files every so often and you will notice that there was much ado about nothing

The unlikely: things happen, but most things do not happen, so why worry about them. Worry about them when they do happen.

The unresolved: many things have no solution, the only action is to manage them when they are around and wait for them to disappear.

Manage yourself:

- Exercise regularly.
- Sleep enough and learn to take naps.

External sources of stress are unavoidable, you have to handle them.
Internal sources of stress, coming from self-inflicted pressure, can be avoided.

THERE IS NO SUCCESS WITHOUT STRESS
THE SECRET LIES IN HANDLING STRESS,
NOT AVOIDING IT

Your notes, thoughts and comments

_____
_____
_____
_____
_____
_____
_____
_____
_____
_____
_____
_____
_____
_____
_____
_____
_____
_____
_____
_____
_____
_____
_____
_____
_____
_____

Tour stop 11

Nothing has broken more careers and made people leave companies than procrastination.

Don't get stuck in perfection: It is better to be roughly right than precisely wrong!!!

Learn to list:

- Positives/Negatives
- Advantages/Disadvantages
- Strengths/Weaknesses
- Good/Bad

And for Pete's sake, make a decision !

The world in general, and the business world in particular, is full of ambiguous, complex and uncertain situations.

You have to have the ability to make effective decisions when there is no one right answer.

Never make a decision yourself that can reasonably be delegated.

Develop a sense of urgency. Decisiveness is a function of urgency.

Urgency is the opposite of:

- Complacency, which is driven by false pride or arrogance.
- Immobilization, which is driven by fear, panic or anger.
- Hesitation, which is driven by pessimism.

LEARN TO BE DECISIVE

Your notes, thoughts and comments

_____

_____

_____

_____

_____

_____

_____

_____

_____

_____

_____

_____

_____

_____

_____

_____

_____

_____

_____

_____

_____

_____

_____

_____

_____

_____

_____

_____

Tour stop 12

No matter how good you are at what you do, no matter how talented, skilled and knowledgeable you are, you need the help and support from mentors.

It is important to have someone pushing you and making you do things you don't think you can do: A mentor moves you from limitation to possibility.

A mentor makes you succeed by making you believe in yourself.

Mentors come in all kind of forms during your life.
You need a mentor at every stage of your life.
You need a mentor at every stage of your career.

What a mentor does for you :

- Serves as confidant in times of personal and professional difficulty.
- Provides feed back on your performance.
- Provides information about the mission, goals and strategic direction of the organization.
- Develops your political awareness and your savvy.
- Provides you with insight into the philosophy or culture of the organization.
- Helps you with your career management.
- Encourages you to take risks and to be involved in visible projects and programs.
- Points out advancement opportunities.

If somebody is prepared to be your mentor, it means you must be exceptional, for only people with potential, people who show promise are being mentored.

Don't wait for mentors to approach you. Dive in your social-network sites and seek them out yourself.

With a little help
from your friends

You need mentors

Your notes, thoughts and comments

_____
_____
_____
_____
_____
_____
_____
_____
_____
_____
_____
_____
_____
_____
_____
_____
_____
_____
_____
_____
_____
_____
_____
_____

MANAGING YOUR BOSS

TOUR STOP 13

If you can't manage your boss, you can't manage subordinates:

- Be professional
- Have the right attitude
- Meet the boss's needs
- Try to make your boss look good
- Be visible
- Take charge
- Communicate well

Communicate regularly and frequently: Be candid always.

Disclose the bad and the ugly, but <u>also</u> the good. You don't want your boss to think of you as a 'bad news person' only.

When you present your boss with a problem, also provide a possible solution; because, if he/she is a good boss, he/she will ask you anyway: What do <u>you</u> think we should do?

If you have the desire to resort to an angry written exchange with your boss, take the time to write your thoughts down ....<u>and don't mail them</u>!!!!

If you feel the need for a verbal argument with your boss, never pick that fight unless you know you can win.

IF YOU CANNOT MANAGE UP,
YOU CANNOT MANAGE DOWN

Your notes, thoughts and comments

_____

_____

_____

_____

_____

_____

_____

_____

_____

_____

_____

_____

_____

_____

_____

_____

_____

_____

_____

_____

_____

_____

_____

_____

TOUR STOP 14

If your boss earned your loyalty, don't ever be disloyal.

Never ever tell your boss' bosses anything, good nor bad, that your boss doesn't already know

Equally, don't work for a boss, who does not grant you access to his/her boss.

Be sensitive to the organizational politics around your boss.

And don't commit social blunders like:

- Criticizing your boss in public.
- Challenging your boss's judgment (his/her mind).
- Becoming known as a naysayer or chronic complainer.
- Being a pest.
- Resisting dress- or demeanor codes.
- Turning down an assignment from top management.
- Burning bridges when you leave an organization.

LOYALTY HAS TO BE EARNED,
IT CANNOT BE COMMANDED

Your notes, thoughts and comments

_____
_____
_____
_____
_____
_____
_____
_____
_____
_____
_____
_____
_____
_____
_____
_____
_____
_____
_____
_____
_____
_____
_____
_____

Tour stop 15

You can be forgiven for almost anything, but you will not be forgiven for spending company money without prior approval from your boss!! It is a capital sin (no pun intended): You will get a death sentence for it!!

If you do not have a thorough understanding of finance and management accounting concepts, you should not be put in a capital spending authority position!

Capital budgeting must be an integral part of your managerial skill set.

DON'T EVER SPEND COMPANY MONEY
WITHOUT YOUR BOSS' APPROVAL

Your notes, thoughts and comments

_____
_____
_____
_____
_____
_____
_____
_____
_____
_____
_____
_____
_____
_____
_____
_____
_____
_____
_____
_____
_____
_____
_____
_____

Tour stop 16

You have to become a participant rather than a target in the appraisal process.

Be prepared, keep a log of your own performance throughout the year and bring it with you.

Get a copy of the appraisal form and fill it out yourself.

Prepare a list of goals and objectives you want to accomplish in the coming year.

Try to anticipate what your boss will tell you and practice your responses.

Participate as an equal partner in the discussion.

Feel free to disagree if the boss is wrong, but take issue with the facts, not with the boss's judgment.

When criticized, own up to the mistakes. Don't get defensive.
Instead, ask how you can improve.

Focus on results. Emphasize the future, not the past.
Listen well and ask questions if you need clarification.

Don't forget to thank your boss for the appraisal.

Follow up on the recommendations.

Don't wait. Ask for it frequently and regularly: "How am I doing?"

Manage your
appraisal process

Your notes, thoughts and comments

_____
_____
_____
_____
_____
_____
_____
_____
_____
_____
_____
_____
_____
_____
_____
_____
_____
_____
_____
_____
_____
_____
_____
_____
_____
_____
_____

Managing your
Subordinate Associates

TOUR STOP 17

What was good for the goose is also good for the gander:

What is the right boss for your subordinate associates to work for?

- A boss who aligns their ambitions with his and with the company's.
- A boss they love to work with and for
- A boss who coaches them.
- A boss they can talk to.
- A boss who is approachable.
- A boss who supports them.
- A boss who delegates to them.
- A boss who trains them, develops them.
- A boss who stretches them.
- A boss who is tough but fair.

If they are going to work for a 'bad boss', once or twice in their career, <u>make sure it is not you</u>.

DON'T WORK FOR THE WRONG BOSS

Your notes, thoughts and comments

_____
_____
_____
_____
_____
_____
_____
_____
_____
_____
_____
_____
_____
_____
_____
_____
_____
_____
_____
_____
_____
_____
_____
_____
_____
_____
_____
_____

TOUR STOP 18

Three things to look for when hiring people:

Integrity: People with integrity tell the truth and keep their word, they take responsibility for past actions, admit mistakes and fix them.

Intelligence: Intelligent people have a strong dose of intellectual curiosity, with breadth of knowledge to work with or lead other smart people.

Maturity: Mature people can withstand pressure, handle stress and setbacks, and – when the moments arise – enjoy success with equal parts of joy and humility.

Three don'ts and one do:

- Don't hire on instinct.
- Don't make hiring decisions based on personal prejudices.
- Don't hire a clone of yourself. You have to surround yourself with people whose skills make up for your own shortcomings.
- Do hire people as good or better as yourself.

Cost effective hiring practices:

- Recommendations from current employees.
- Referral bonuses to current employees.
- Recruiting from within.
- Rehiring former employees.

In the end, when you have more than one great candidate, when all else is equal, always choose the person who wants the job more.

Hiring people is easy
Hiring good people is tough
Hiring great people is
extraordinary difficult

Your notes, thoughts and comments

_____

_____

_____

_____

_____

_____

_____

_____

_____

_____

_____

_____

_____

_____

_____

_____

_____

_____

_____

_____

_____

_____

_____

_____

TOUR STOP 19

According to various studies, 50 to 60% of employees change jobs in the first seven months of employment. As soon as they are hired they start looking for better opportunities.

Why? Because of a lack of proper introduction:

- Do I feel welcome and valued here?
- In what way is my job important to this organization?
- Exactly what is expected of me?
- Will I learn, grow and be challenged here?
- Will I get to exercise independent judgment and creativity?

Letting new arrivals linger, making them hang around, letting them find out for themselves, having them fend for themselves, is not the right way to getting people off to a great start.

The people who have been assigned to correctly manage the initial joining-up process have to be available, which all too often they are not.

First impressions are deep impressions. They are difficult to undo.
Manage them well.

FIRST IMPRESSIONS
ARE DEEP IMPRESSIONS

Your notes, thoughts and comments

_____
_____
_____
_____
_____
_____
_____
_____
_____
_____
_____
_____
_____
_____
_____
_____
_____
_____
_____
_____
_____
_____
_____
_____
_____
_____
_____

Tour stop 20

How people are paid is often more important than how much they are paid.

If the perceived value of the compensation does not exceed the cost, it is not a good deal, not for the employee or for the company.

The best way to make compensation value exceed its cost is to combine financial and non-financial rewards.

Compensation has to be tied to performance.

That performance has to be based on contribution, not on seniority, not on rank.

That performance has to be objectively measurable.

Leadership, customer service and profits should be the main categories of measurement.

Compensation can only achieve so much. Money is important,

However, it is not the only thing that motivates people.

When salary and benefits are fair, most people value intangible benefits more:

- Flexible work schedules
- Company-provided Blackberry's and cell phones
- Career growth and learning.
- Exciting, challenging and meaningful work.
- The opportunity to make a difference.
- A great boss and great co-workers and social interaction.
- Recognition for a job well done.
- Having fun on the job.
- Autonomy and a sense of control over their own work.
- Unpaid leave, a gap break.

Ownership is a strong motivator: Give employees a stake in the company's success.

NOT ENOUGH MONEY
IS A STRONG DE-MOTIVATOR

THE PROSPECT OF MORE MONEY
IS A POWERFUL MOTIVATOR

PAID MONEY IS SUNK
AND IS TAKEN FOR GRANTED

Your notes, thoughts and comments

_____
_____
_____
_____
_____
_____
_____
_____
_____
_____
_____
_____
_____
_____
_____
_____
_____
_____
_____
_____
_____

Tour stop 21

The biggest cause they want to work for is the fulfillment of their desire for achievement.

If the company is seen to fulfill that desire for achievement, they will work for the company.

If you personally are seen to fulfill that desire for achievement, they will work for you.

Desire for achievement comes in many forms:

Desire for activity:

- Make work more active, build fun into the work.
- Add variety to work, ask for employee input.

Desire for power:

- Give employees responsibility for their work.
- Provide leadership opportunities.

Desire for competence and self-development:

- Use employee's strengths.
- Provide learning opportunities.
- Tolerate mistakes.

Desire for accomplishment:

- Provide objective performance measures.
- Let employees set goals for themselves.
- Encourage employees to improve.
- Challenge employees to stretch their limits.

PEOPLE WANT TO WORK
FOR A CAUSE NOT JUST FOR A LIVING

Your notes, thoughts and comments

_____

_____

_____

_____

_____

_____

_____

_____

_____

_____

_____

_____

_____

_____

_____

_____

_____

_____

_____

_____

_____

_____

_____

_____

_____

Tour stop 22

It is difficult, if not impossible, to be important totally on your own:

People come to work for social interaction, for a social identity.

People come to work for camaraderie, to work with their friends.

People have a desire for affiliation and involvement; they want to be part of a group, part of a team.

- Offer opportunities to socialize and use the power of teamwork.
- Offer recognition, respect and dignity.

The value of titles is underestimated. Titles don't cost anything.
Status symbols are important.

Use both wisely. Proliferation brings the value down.

Managing people is more than managing individuals:
It is also managing the relationships among people.

PEOPLE WANT TO FEEL IMPORTANT
MAKE THEM FEEL IMPORTANT

Your notes, thoughts and comments

_____
_____
_____
_____
_____
_____
_____
_____
_____
_____
_____
_____
_____
_____
_____
_____
_____
_____
_____
_____
_____
_____
_____
_____
_____
_____
_____
_____

TOUR STOP 23

One sure way of motivating people is to eliminate de-motivators. There is no lack of choice:

- Office politics
- Unclear expectations
- Unnecessary rules
- Poorly designed work processes
- Unproductive meetings
- Lack of follow up
- Constant Change
- Internal competition
- Dishonesty
- Hypocrisy
- Discouraging responses
- Criticism
- Underutilization
- Tolerating poor performance
- Being taken for granted
- Over-control
- Unfairness
- Being forced to do poor quality work
- …

MANAGEMENT IS REMOVING OBSTACLES

Your notes, thoughts and comments

_____
_____
_____
_____
_____
_____
_____
_____
_____
_____
_____
_____
_____
_____
_____
_____
_____
_____
_____
_____
_____
_____
_____
_____
_____

Tour stop 24

Trust greases the wheels of your success.

How, where and when you say something is as important as what you say.

Communicate what and why to everyone, never only to the favored few.

Keep it short, keep it focused, keep it simple.

Communication is a two-way process that involves knowing how to receive, as well as how to give information. Learn to listen.

Your ability to communicate effectively depends largely on your reputation and credibility. People won't believe what you tell them if they think you are dishonest and manipulative.

Be frank about problems, acknowledge difficulties, even failures.

If you try to avoid discussing them, people will think you have a hidden agenda or are trying to manipulate them.

If you communicate criticism, don't address a group. The group will gang up on you.

What you say and what is heard are often not the same.
Try important messages out on a small select group first, and check if what you want to say is the same as what is heard.

Avoid information overload.

Communication is not only about the spoken or written word. It is also about your facial expressions, your body language, the image you project. Often it is more about what you do than what you say.

MAKE THEM TRUST YOU

Your notes, thoughts and comments

_____
_____
_____
_____
_____
_____
_____
_____
_____
_____
_____
_____
_____
_____
_____
_____
_____
_____
_____
_____
_____
_____
_____
_____
_____
_____
_____
_____
_____
_____
_____
_____

Tour stop 25

Effective managers get things done through other people: They empower members of their team by giving them tasks and the authority to get them done, and by holding them accountable for their successful completion.

Effective delegators never abdicate responsibility. They merely respect the knowledge of their people and let them use it.

Abdicators on the other hand, give away their accountability. As a result, team members may feel out on a limb or in over their heads.

Frustration mounts, and people blame the leader for a lack of support, ambiguous authority and absentee monitoring.

Two wrong fears why managers don't delegate:

'I need to be visible': Correct, except you need to be 'visible' but only as someone who is an excellent delegator!!

'I am going to be replaced': Correct again, except you want to be replaced … to be promoted!!

Some lame and feeble excuses for not delegating:

- It takes longer to explain than do the job.
- Employee mistakes are costly.
- As a manager I get things done quicker.
- My employees are not ready for more responsibilities.
- When I delegate I lose control.
- I like to make my own decisions.

Management Isn't Doing - It's Seeing That Things Get Done

Your notes, thoughts and comments

_____
_____
_____
_____
_____
_____
_____
_____
_____
_____
_____
_____
_____
_____
_____
_____
_____
_____
_____
_____
_____
_____
_____
_____
_____
_____
_____
_____
_____

Tour stop 26

Delegate anything that is reasonably possible.

Don't delegate everything:

- Don't delegate employee selection more than is absolutely necessary.
- Don't delegate hiring, compensating, motivating, assessing and firing of your direct reports
- Don't delegate those decisions which have the greatest impact on the organization.
- Don't delegate the resolution of disputes between your direct reports

Your direct reports should from time to time find that decisions are taken from them.

This helps clarify that authority flows from the top down and exists by the grace of you.

Sometimes, a little lesson in humility is good for everybody.

What not to delegate:

Planning and Forecasting
Personnel matters

Your notes, thoughts and comments

_____
_____
_____
_____
_____
_____
_____
_____
_____
_____
_____
_____
_____
_____
_____
_____
_____
_____
_____
_____
_____
_____
_____
_____
_____
_____

TOUR STOP 27

I can live for two months on a good compliment (Mark Twain)

Recognition:

Do it often
Do it swiftly
Praise individuals, not teams
Do it proportionately
Tailor it
Think small

Recognition tools:

Write a quick thank-you note

Write your boss a memo and copy your employee

Introduce employee to a visitor

Buy the employee coffee or lunch

POWERFUL TWO WORD COMBINATIONS WITH HIGH VALUE AND ZERO COST:

THANK YOU
WELL DONE
GREAT JOB

Your notes, thoughts and comments

_____
_____
_____
_____
_____
_____
_____
_____
_____
_____
_____
_____
_____
_____
_____
_____
_____
_____
_____

Tour stop 28

Why good people leave:

- They see no link between their pay and their performance.
- They don't perceive growth or advancement opportunities.
- They don't see their work as important, or their contributions are not recognized.
- They don't get to use their natural talents.
- They have unclear or unrealistic expectations.
- They will no longer tolerate abusive managers or toxic environments.
- The job was not as expected.
- Mismatch between job and person.
- Too little coaching and feedback.
- Stress from overwork and work-life imbalance.
- Loss of trust in senior management.

FIRING PEOPLE IS A LUXURY
GOOD PEOPLE OFTEN LEAVE

Your notes, thoughts and comments

_____
_____
_____
_____
_____
_____
_____
_____
_____
_____
_____
_____
_____
_____
_____
_____
_____
_____
_____
_____
_____
_____
_____
_____
_____
_____
_____
_____
_____
_____

Tour stop 29

Challenge yourself:

- Did the employee know his or her performance was unacceptable? No surprises.
- Was the employee given a fair chance to improve?
- Can you prove it? (And is it properly documented?)
- Does there appear to be a non-performance reason? (For which you could be possibly responsible?)

Managers often get firing wrong for two reasons:

- Moving too fast.
- Taking too long.

Of the two reasons the latter is by far the worst.

But, if you are agonizing over whether to fire someone or not:
Do it and Do it quickly!!

When firing, choose the time carefully
- Minimize humiliation, build up a person's self-confidence.
- Get right to the point.
- Don't be brutal, focus on the problem, not on the person.
- When the employee reacts, don't argue, just listen.
- Like any other form of communication, keep it short, keep it focused, keep it simple.

Before firing an employee:
Challenge yourself

Your notes, thoughts and comments

_____
_____
_____
_____
_____
_____
_____
_____
_____
_____
_____
_____
_____
_____
_____
_____
_____
_____
_____
_____
_____
_____
_____
_____
_____
_____
_____
_____

Tour stop 30

<u>The Unable and unwilling.</u> (the bottom 5%)

Terminate immediately, they have to go!! Why were they hired in the first place?
Review your hiring processes.

<u>The able but unwilling.</u> (Toxic combination!!)

Question: Why are they unwilling?
Answer: Low self-esteem, fear, resentment, boredom, unresolved conflict?
Can it be rectified quickly to enable transition to 'willing'?
If not, don't hesitate: Terminate them.

<u>The willing and able</u> (the top 20%)

Train them, improve them, delegate to them, challenge them, stretch them, promote them.

These people have to be showered with bonuses, stock options, praise and a variety of rewards to their pocketbooks and souls.

<u>The willing but semi-able</u> (70%)

Manage and motivate them, they are the majority of your employees.

Don't take them for granted, they are the heart and soul of your company.

Training-Training-Training.

Try to move them into the top 20%.

Know your people

The willing and able (20%)
The willing and semi-able (70%)
The able and unwilling (5%)
The unable and unwilling (5%)

Your notes, thoughts and comments

_____
_____
_____
_____
_____
_____
_____
_____
_____
_____
_____
_____
_____
_____
_____
_____
_____
_____
_____
_____

Managing Colleagues and Stakeholders

Tour stop 31

Are you a person with a captivating, charming and inspiring personality who attracts the attention, affections and respect of others?

Charisma is not a substitute for talent, knowledge, managerial skills or work ethic, but it surely helps to amplify and enlarge competence.

A little extravagance and flamboyance don't hurt.
Be a charming deviationist.

How is your handshake? Is it firm, dry and memorable?
Can you sustain eye contact?
Do you remember names well?
Do you have a sense of humor and do you know how to use it effectively?
Can you laugh at yourself? A bit of self-deprecating humor is welcome.
Do you know how to deal with a bit of silliness, even a bit of irreverence?
Do you know how to give compliments that are tactful, sensible and credible?
Do you know that listening intently is one of the greatest forms of effective flattery?

Do you have the personal warmth to be approachable? Is your mood consistent?

How are you with empathy? Do you sense others' emotions, understand their perspective and take active interest in their perspective? Are you sensitive to other people's feelings?

Are you in tune to the currents and politics of your company?

Do you have access to your boss' boss? Do you know his lateral colleagues?

Do you know the names, the backgrounds and the performance of all the people which report to your direct reports?

Personal warmth
Sensitivity

Your notes, thoughts and comments

_____
_____
_____
_____
_____
_____
_____
_____
_____
_____
_____
_____
_____
_____
_____
_____
_____
_____
_____
_____
_____
_____
_____
_____
_____

Tour stop 32

Manage, don't plan, your career.

It is good to be:

- enterprising
- aspiring
- desiring
- eager
- hopeful
- purposeful

However, it is not good to be blindly, thoughtlessly ambitious:

You won't get there anyway, somebody sometime somewhere will stop you, and even if you do get there, it will never be far enough, you will never be satisfied and happy and you will make everybody else around you miserable too.

Don't keep your eye on the next promotion, on the next job, instead keep your nose to the grindstone, do your work well, work hard and look for more work all the time. Focus on exercising your abilities. Using your talents in work you enjoy will often bring more satisfaction than a new title.

Relax a bit, feel at ease, let life unfold itself, let life surprise you.

Always be prepared to take advantage of the unfolding surprises and go with the flow.

WHAT YOU THINK
YOUR FUTURE SHOULD BE
IS NOT THE SAME AS
WHAT YOUR DESTINY WILL BE

Your notes, thoughts and comments

_____
_____
_____
_____
_____
_____
_____
_____
_____
_____
_____
_____
_____
_____
_____
_____
_____
_____
_____
_____
_____
_____
_____
_____

Tour stop 33

Fear of your own success is as powerful and as devastating as fear of failure.

Fear of your own success is as common as fear of failure.

Both sabotage your career.

Career sabotage for fear of failure can be repaired.

Career sabotage for fear of your own success is usually fatal and finite.

Common forms of career sabotage:

- Overstretching of power and prerogatives: misappropriation of company resources.
- Failure to delegate, which causes severe work overload and alienates subordinates.
- Over-delegation and abdication is the same as appearing idle and superfluous.
- Inability to make key decisions when the stakes are high.
- Greed, engaging in ethical or legal violations, asking for kickbacks.
- Political blundering, bypassing your boss, criticizing your boss in public.
- Overt disloyalty to your company or boss.
- Burning bridges when you leave a boss, a department or the organization.

Common forms of self-sabotage:

- Excessive drinking: causes lateness and absenteeism, chronic fatigue, mood swings
- Drug abuse: risk of mental and physical problems, impaired judgment.
- Compulsive spending: it creates debt, worry, distraction and poor job performance.

There are more ways to sabotage a career than to make a career.

IT IS NOT NECESSARY
TO BE AN IDIOT
TO ACT LIKE A FOOL

Your notes, thoughts and comments

_____

_____

_____

_____

_____

_____

_____

_____

_____

_____

_____

_____

_____

_____

_____

_____

_____

_____

_____

_____

_____

_____

_____

_____

Tour Stop 34

You have to be successful in all aspects:

- In your career/profession
- With your health and condition
- With your family

What kind of a husband or spouse are you?
What kind of a father or mother are you?
What kind of a grandfather/grandmother are you?

What kind of a Work-Life balance do you have?

- Your priorities and values
- Your choices
- Your trade-offs

Even the most accommodating bosses believe that Work-Life balance is <u>your</u> problem to solve.

YOU ARE NOT SUCCESSFUL
UNTIL/UNLESS
YOU ARE SUCCESSFUL
IN <u>ALL</u> ASPECTS OF YOUR LIFE

Your notes, thoughts and comments

_____
_____
_____
_____
_____
_____
_____
_____
_____
_____
_____
_____
_____
_____
_____
_____
_____
_____
_____
_____
_____
_____
_____
_____
_____

UP THE LADDER

If you have worked your way up the ladder and you have people managers reporting to you, always ask yourself this simple question about any of these individuals: If I were younger and/or less senior again, would I mind reporting to this person? If the answer is 'absolutely not', ask yourself urgently this second question: Why then should I have anybody else in my organization report to that person?

The first is a straightforward and fair question. The second, if it needs to be asked, is an uncomfortable question. But it is still a good question!

*

At the lower echelon, your best worker is not necessarily a good supervisor. Keep that in mind when you are thinking of promotion. You may lose your best worker and acquire your worst supervisor.

That principle works at every sport of the ladder, all the way to the top: Your best performing VP is not necessarily a good Senior VP.

There is a big difference between rewarding performance and promoting managerial capabilities. If you can combine the two successfully, you've got a winner. If you combine them unsuccessfully, you've got two losers on your hand.

*

The 'promotor' and 'promotee' share equal responsibility for making a promotion succeed, the former for offering and the latter for accepting the advancement. The former should not offer carelessly, neither should the latter accept lightly.

*

Two important reasons to manage and to treat people well: It is in the roam of possibilities that some day you may report to someone who, at some time in the past, reported to you or was a colleague. Secondly, a career is not always on the up and up. Sometimes, because of reasons out of your control (like acquisition or divestment …) it is not inconceivable that you may have to take a step down, at which time you may meet people you met on the way up.

CLOSE ENCOUNTERS

OF SOME KIND...

... with the first man in my life

My grandfather on mother's side worked 38 years underground in the coalmine before he retired. My grandfather on father's side also was a coalminer for 37 years. All my great uncles and uncles worked underground. My father worked **on** the mine, not **in** the mine. So that was a first departure away from the underground. He was a manager, an excellent people manager. That was the second departure.

He was of course never going to let his son go back in the other direction. Imagine his horror when his son of sixteen tells him that he is no longer interested in studying, that mathematics is all too difficult and that he rather would work in the coalmine.

Good, said my father, *but before you make that decision, maybe you should work during your vacation and if you really like it, then, after your vacation, you can let me know and I will get you a job in the mine. Is that a deal?*

Ok, yes, that was a fair deal, I thought.

Dad had many professional connections. He knew a man, Jean was his name, who owned a cement factory, where they poured heavy concrete construction materials. The factory was mostly open air manufacturing. Dad, of course, had a quiet little word with this Jean and undoubtedly gave him instructions to figuratively break this 16-year old boy's back.

It was a lousy rotten summer, cold and lots of rain, and Jean made me load and unload trucks all day, from morning till closing time.. If anybody was going to break my back, he could do it. I managed to keep up, with great courage, for six weeks. By that time I was so empty and had lost so much weight, that I was beginning to look like a skeleton. But my pride stood in the way of reason and I kept going until one morning at six o'clock I could no longer get out of bed. I was a boy running on empty, there was nothing left, I was totally depleted.

But here came my father onto my room:

Get up Cyriel, it is time to go to work!

No, I can't get up

What do you mean, you can't get up? I am up, am I not?

Yes, but I just can't get up anymore?

So let us be clear, you are sixteen, you have only 49 years more to work before you retire and you can't get up? You can't be serious!!!

I am not going to go to work!!

Today only? or not any more?

Not any more!!

OK, so what do you plan to do then?

I'll go back to school.

OK, I agree with that, I will talk to Jean, I am sure he will accept your resignation. I have to go to work now so that you can go back to school, you understand that? Do you appreciate that now?

Yes.

Good, sleep well then.

It is one of the only conversations with my father that I remember. But I have to admit, if he ever was going to have a conversation with his oldest, this was the very one to have.

As I stated, without luck nothing much is possible.

… with a numbers man.

I went back to school but I was a rebel. In 1962 I incurred Saturday detention 30 times. This seemed quite excessive until I found out later that my mathematics teacher, Professor Claes, had instructed all his colleagues to 'catch me if they could' and impose the maximum Saturday detention. Since I got in trouble every day at least once, this was not a tall order.

Professor Claes was a priest of the old fashioned school, black frock, completely smudged with white chalk from writing his hieroglyphics on the blackboard. He smoked big cigars and smelled like one. He had a very loud roaring laugh that he let loose every time one of his students made a mistake. To this day, when I think of that laugh I still get a sinking feeling. On Saturday he read his breviary and he obviously liked my company while doing that.

Every Saturday morning at nine he was present in the classroom waiting for his favorite. He would sit at his high desk in front of the blackboard. I would sit on the first desk right in front of him. Here was the routine:

OK, James Dean, you know the rules. I give you three problems. If you give me the right solutions your detention is over and you can go and chase the girls. For every wrong answer though, I will give you three new problems. The day can be short or it can be long, it is up to you!!

He would start with two easy problems to encourage me and one difficult one to floor me. He had two pens, a blue for the correct answers and a red for the wrong ones. Number one, good, in blue, number two, good, in blue, number three … ah! and here came that loud roaring laugh and the red pen …. Before he would send me back to my desk with the obligatory three new problems, he would give me a piece of chalk and made me show him on the blackboard where the mistake was made.

For every wrong one, three new problems, that was the rule. He covered all the fields from Algebra to Geometry to Trigonometry to Analytical Geometry to Pre-Calculus. I never left the class room before five in the evening. When he noticed I became better at it, he increased the difficulty level, just to make sure I had at least always three new problems ahead of me.

In the meantime he would read his breviary and mumble. After lunch (my mother made sandwiches for the two of us) he would light a cigar and smile at me benignly and with delight. What a wonderful Saturday!

When the last Saturday before the exams came about, he was there at nine. He gave me three problems. I solved them in five minutes. He got his blue pen out and never bothered with the red one. But he laughed nevertheless, a long hearty laugh.

Alright, James Dean, you can go!!

I passed the exams with flying colors. I had become numerate. On the 29th of June, 1964, I ended my high school days as the first of my class.

It is easier with a little help from your friends.

… with a mentor

As a younger manager at the middle echelon of my career, I had the good fortune to report directly to the Chief Executive Officer of the company. The Brussels location, of which I was the general manager, was the company's first distribution center on the European Continent, was advanced in its innovative lay-out and was developing the first information technology directed inventory and picking systems. It called for the attention of the very top man himself and I happened to be the lucky one to benefit from it.

He used to fly from Edinburgh into Brussels every three weeks on the company plane to come and check on the progress. I would be waiting for him at the airport, always a bit nervous, always well prepared. He would greet me with "hello young man", which today sounds strange to me, but back then, I guess, I was indeed a young man.

I always kept the very highest housekeeping standards in the warehouse for I was a great believer in the fact that the housekeeping benchmark is a measure of the management quality. For his three-weekly visit one literally 'could eat from the floor'!! This pleased my big boss no end, but still, if required, he would crawl on hands and knees under the racking to find something, to retrieve a piece of wood or paper or any kind of trash. *Ha, ha*! he would say, very pleased with himself, *I found something*!!!

In de car on the way back to the airport I once objected: *Sir, I was in the X. warehouse last week. That warehouse was not up to snuff!! Why do you crawl on your hands and knees under the racking to find that exceptional piece of litter? Why do you keep me to such a different standard?*

He said: *You see, young man, the manager at X. is not very good, he will not go anywhere, he will not get any better and he will probably not last in the company. I am not going to put my time into him. You on the other hand, you are going to go places, you are good but you can still get a lot better. That is why I keep you to a different standard, because I know that next time it is going to be even better. I do not get on my hands and knees to be hard to please, I get on my hands and my knees to make you a better manager*!!!

It is a lot easier with the help of a mentor.

... with a stranger in the night

I was on my way to the UK, flying through the night, on British Airways, for a board meeting in London. Next to me, separated by the aisle, was a little, middle aged woman. She had a pretty, round, expressive face, short hair. From her accent I could make out that she was Dutch.

After the meal we introduced ourselves and we got talking. She asked all there is to know about me, my job and my life. She told me about her and her life, like two strangers in the night.

She was on a return flight to London, where she lived. She had just been visiting with her daughter in NY. Her husband had been a very big shot in a global Dutch electronics company. He had died a year earlier. Leslie was a widow.

Well, it seems that your husband was a very successful man, I said.

No, she said, *he was not. In order to be successful you have to be successful in all aspects of your life. My husband was a most excellent business man and top manager, he was a wonderful husband and father, but he did not take care of his health, he did not exercise, he drank too much at his business lunches and dinners and he smoked himself to death. He died of lung cancer. If my husband had been successful in every aspect of his life, then he would still be alive, our daughter would still have a father and I would not be a widow. He is no longer here and therefore he was not successful.*

That made a deep impression on me and it made me silent for a while.

She remained quiet as well to let her words sink in. Then she looked over at me and put her hand across the aisle on my forearm and said: *you, Mr. Godderie, are not a very successful man either!! You are a successful manager, you take good care of yourself, you bike extensively, you don't smoke, you keep your weight in check and you don't drink excessively, but you are a distant husband and an absent father. Successful men are successful in every aspect of their lives and you are not. Like my husband you are not a successful man!!*

I picked up her hand from my arm and kissed it. She smiled and withdrew it gently. She said, *I guess your kiss means that you forgive me for what I said. For my husband it is all too late, but you have the rest of your life to become a successful man.*

After that we both reclined our seats and went to sleep.

Thank you, Leslie. Wherever you are, I wished you could know that I became an ever present, very close grandfather. I can obviously not undo the past, but I can certainly do the future.

There is a time to be successful in life. There is a time to make a success of your life.

ABOUT THE TOUR GUIDE

Cyriel Godderie has had a life long interest and fascination with intercultural adaptation and perspective. Born in Belgium in 1945, a country torn apart by cultural and linguistic infighting, as a 23 year young man of Flemish origin, he voluntarily chose to fulfill his military duties in a French speaking battalion, where, as one Fleming amongst some 800 Walloon soldiers he discovered the immense power of transcending cultural divide. It was to be a life changing experience that put him on the way to a successful international and multinational career.

Cyriel studied Modern Languages and Business Administration. He graduated as Interpreter in Dutch, English, French and German. He complemented his formal education with extensive private Management courses at the University of Ghent and Management Accounting at the University of Louvain. He widened his language skills to Italian, in which he developed excellent understanding and reading ability.

Cyriel pursued a life long career in Logistics and Supply Chain Management. In 2000 he reached the pinnacle of his career when he was appointed CEO and Chairman, in which capacity he was responsible for 123 logistics sites in the USA and 10 countries in Europe, totaling a turnover of 750 million dollars and 7500 employees, with regional head offices in NJ (where he resides), London, Paris and Helsingborg. On the way to the summit he passed, from the bottom up, through all the various stages of promotion in operating hands-on-management positions. He managed huge dedicated logistics contracts with world class customers like Marks and Spencer, the Kroger Company, The Campbell Soup, just to name a few.

SOME EXCELLENT BOOKS
FOR THE STUDIOUS READER

BIBLIOGRAPHY

Embracing Excellence – Franklin C Ashly, Arthur R. Pell

Getting a grip on tomorrow – Mike Johnson

Getting a project done on time – Paul B. Williams

Keeping the people who keep you in business – Leigh Branham

Managing your mind – Gillian Butler, Tony Hope

Rewards that drive high performance – Thomas B. Wilson

Stop managing, start coaching – Jerry W Gilley, Nathaniel W. Broughton

Supermotivation – Dean R. Spitzer

Survival skills for a reengineered world – William N. Yeomans

The leader in you – Stuart R. Levine, Michael A Crom

The hidden reasons employees leave – Leigh Branham

The bad attitude survival guide – Harry E Chambers

Winning – Jack Welch and Suzy Welch

Your own worst enemy – Andrew J. Dubrin

Printed in the United States
by Baker & Taylor Publisher Services